Contents

Health, Nutrition, and P.E. PreK–K, SV 141902356X

Introduction

The school curriculum designates the topics taught to students. Health is one of the subjects that teachers should target. However, most stress is put on the core subjects, which leaves little time for this important area. An increased interest in the health of Americans has led to a revised interest in promoting health in the classroom.

Research suggests that the greatest threats to the health of Americans today are lifestyle diseases, such as cardiovascular disease and cancer. Among children, injuries claim more lives than disease. The facts that determine the length and quality of an individual's life are most often personal choices in several areas: diet, exercise, and personal cleanliness; the use of tobacco, alcohol, and other drugs; and the application of new health information to one's own habits. Responsibility for maintaining health and for minimizing the risk of developing chronic and degenerative diseases and disorders rests with the individual and begins early in life.

To achieve this goal, health education should promote positive attitudes, consistent positive behaviors, and good decision-making skills, which will contribute to good health and long-range prevention of disease. Effective health education should combine content and skill practice in a meaningful way that is applicable to daily life. Thus, health education is really life education. *Health, Nutrition, and P.E.* provides content and skills practice that will benefit all children. The activity pages address health concepts that can be applied on a personal level.

Organization

Health, Nutrition, and P.E. is divided into three units.

- **Unit 1** provides information on growth, the body, hygiene, drugs, and safety practices.
- **Unit 2** introduces information on nutrition. It includes background about the new Food Pyramid and healthy food selections.
- **Unit 3** explores fitness and exercise concepts. It offers activity pages explaining the benefits of exercise as well as specific, hands-on exercise suggestions.

Additional Notes

- **Health Skills Observation Checklist** Page 3 offers a list of healthy behaviors that prekindergarten and kindergarten children should be able to master. You may wish to copy the list for each child and note the date when a behavior is exhibited.

- **Teacher Resource** Each unit begins with an introduction. It provides background information important to completing some of the skill pages as well as gives an overview of the concepts children will explore.

- **Books** A list of books, both fiction and nonfiction, is provided for each unit to further expose children to the health concepts introduced in this book.

- **Bulletin Board** A bulletin board idea accompanies each unit. The idea is either child-created or interactive, which meets standards required for classroom decoration. Detailed instructions explain how to build the board. Patterns are also provided.

- **Lesson Plans** *Health, Nutrition, and P.E.* offers 25 hands-on lesson plans to explicitly teach important health concepts. Each lesson identifies the corresponding health standards, the materials, explicit instructions, and a song or poem to reinforce the skill.

- **Picture Cards and Patterns** Some lessons require materials to facilitate discussion or build concrete understanding. These resources are included after the lesson plans and are noted in the materials list.

- **Activity Master** An activity master that reinforces the health concept is included in each lesson.

- **Booklets** Five booklets can be copied and distributed to children. The booklets emphasize important health concepts and skills. You may wish to encourage children to take them home to share with family members.

Health Skills Observation Checklist

Child's Name _____ **Date** _____

RATING SCALE

| **3** Outstanding | **2** Satisfactory | **1** Improvement Needed | ☐ Not Enough Opportunity to Observe |

Makes Decisions	**Comments**
☐ considers options, risks, and constraints	
☐ role-plays healthful decision-making skills	
☐ makes wise decisions in everyday situations	
Exhibits Refusal Skills	
☐ says "no" in a convincing way	
☐ suggests healthful alternatives to health-risking activities	
☐ uses facts to explain reasons for refusal	
☐ walks away if peer pressure becomes too great	
Resolves Conflicts	
☐ explores options	
☐ listens attentively to others	
☐ deals with a problem calmly or makes plans to discuss the problem at a later time	
☐ walks away when a situation becomes violent	
Manages Stress	
☐ recognizes the cause of stress	
☐ discusses feelings and seeks help if necessary	
☐ finds an outlet to reduce stress, such as exercise	
Communicates	
☐ organizes ideas logically	
☐ presents ideas clearly	
☐ fulfills the purpose of the communication	
☐ listens attentively to others	
Sets Goals	
☐ sets reasonable goals to improve or maintain health	
☐ makes an action plan to achieve goals	
☐ follows a plan	
☐ evaluates the results of personal efforts	

Health Skills Observation Checklist
Health, Nutrition, and P.E. PreK–K, SV 141902356X

Health Awards

Wow, _____!
child's name

**You are BLASTING OFF to good
health because you**

_____.

Clang, clang, _____!
child's name

You are on track with good food because you

_____.

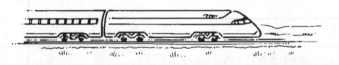

Good job, _____!
child's name

You are building a strong body because you

_____.

Health Awards
Health, Nutrition, and P.E. PreK–K, SV 141902356X

Teacher Resource

Health for children revolves around a basic understanding of the functions of the human body and good health practices. By learning about their body, children can more easily understand why they should make healthy choices. It is never too early to begin healthy habits in hygiene, drugs, and safety. The habits they form will affect their life for many years to come.

Body Systems

There are twelve systems that work together to form the most amazing machine—the human body. Young children should be introduced to different parts of the body and how they work. They should also learn the names and functions of the most important organs, including the sensing body parts, bones, and the heart. All twelve systems are briefly described on this page and on page 6.

Skeletal System   The adult skeleton is a framework of 206 bones that fit together. It holds up the body and gives it shape. It also protects the internal organs and allows the body to move.

Muscular System   This system is made up of more than 600 muscles whose primary job is to move the body by contraction, or pulling. There are two main kinds of muscles: skeletal muscles and smooth muscles. Skeletal muscles, also known as voluntary muscles, are connected to the bones and can consciously be controlled. Smooth muscles, or involuntary muscles, contract automatically. The heart is a third kind of muscle, known as the cardiac muscle.

Digestive System   Digestion is the process by which food is broken down into particles, which provide energy and nutrients needed by the body to function. Digestion begins in the mouth, where teeth break the food. Saliva moistens it and begins the chemical breakdown. The food moves through the esophagus and then into the stomach, where it is broken down into a liquid. The food then moves into the small intestine, where acids and enzymes further process the food into substances for the body's use. Waste products are then moved through the large intestine.

Respiratory System   The respiratory system is responsible for breathing. Its main functions are to take in oxygen and remove carbon dioxide. Air enters the body through the nose and moves through the bronchial tubes into the lungs.

Circulatory System   This system moves blood throughout the body. Blood is essential since it carries food and oxygen for life, as well as removes carbon dioxide and wastes. The heart is the most important organ in this system.

Lymphatic System   This system works in conjunction with the circulatory system. Many white blood cells are found in the lymph nodes and are responsible for protecting the body from disease.

Reproductive System   The reproductive organs allow humans to have children. A sperm cell from a male joins with an egg cell from a female to produce a fertilized egg that develops into a human being.

Urinary System   In this system, liquid wastes are removed from the body. Blood moves through two kidneys that filter out water with other particles. The water travels through tubes to be excreted in the form of urine.

Endocrine System   The endocrine system of glands produces a variety of hormones that regulate growth, reproduction, and food use.

Nervous System   This system is responsible for controlling and coordinating all the systems in the body. The brain is the nerve center that receives and understands messages. It reacts and tells the body what to do. The five senses fall under this system.

Integumentary System   The integumentary system is made up of the skin, hair, nails, and sweat glands. The skin is actually an organ and is the largest one in the body.

Immune System   This system protects the body from disease. Organs, tissues, cells, and secretions from a variety of the body's systems play a role in immunity.

Staying Healthy

Staying healthy involves many factors, from making good, healthful choices in hygiene to visiting doctors on a regular basis for checkups and vaccine maintenance.

Hygiene   Hygiene involves keeping the body clean. For elementary students, stress should be placed on personal cleanliness, including dental and body care.

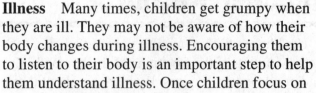

Routine habits developed at a young age can prevent many health problems later in life.

Illness   Many times, children get grumpy when they are ill. They may not be aware of how their body changes during illness. Encouraging them to listen to their body is an important step to help them understand illness. Once children focus on how their body changes when they are ill, they should be given a vocabulary to communicate their illness.

Drugs   For children, the word *drug* is often presented in the context of a harmful substance to be avoided. However, prescribed and over-the-counter medicines are drugs, too. A distinction should be made between healthful medicines, given by doctors and trusted adults, and harmful chemicals. In early elementary grades, discussion should be about harmful chemicals, which include tobacco and alcohol.

Safety

Young children can begin to understand many kinds of safety practices and the steps that should be followed for each. From the beginning, children should learn specific emergency information, including how to dial 911 and information to share when reporting an emergency. Other important safety subjects include fire, sun, and bike safety.

Health, Nutrition, and P.E. PreK–K, SV 141902356X

Health Books

Senses

The Five Senses by Keith Faulkner (Cartwheel Books)

Is It Rough? Is It Smooth? Is It Shiny? by Tana Hoban (Greenwillow)

My Five Senses by Aliki (HarperCollins)

You Can't Smell a Flower with Your Ear by Joanna Cole (Grosset & Dunlap)

Body

Me and My Amazing Body by Joan Sweeney (Dragonfly)

My First Body Book by Christopher Rice (DK Publishing)

The Skeleton Inside You by Philip Balestrino (HarperTrophy)

Two Eyes, a Nose, and a Mouth by Roberta Grobel Intrater (Scholastic, Inc.)

Your Skin and Mine by Paul Showers (HarperCollins)

Hygiene and General Health Practices

Achoo: All About Colds by Patricia Demuth (Grosset & Dunlap)

Brush Your Teeth Please by Leslie McGuire (Reader's Digest)

Feelings by Aliki (Greenwillow)

I Am a Doctor by Cynthia Benjamin (Barron's Educational Series)

I Wish Daddy Didn't Drink So Much by Judith Vigna (Albert Whitman Company)

Little Bear Brushes His Teeth by Jutta Langreuter and Vera Sobat (The Millbrook Press)

Pooh Plays Doctor by Kathleen Soehfeld (Disney Press)

Safety

Dinosaurs, Beware! A Safety Guide by Marc Brown and Stephen Krensky (Little, Brown, and Company)

I Am Fire by Jean Marzollo (Cartwheel Books)

Stitches by Harriet Ziefert (Puffin Books)

Health, Nutrition, and P.E. PreK–K, SV 141902356X

Bulletin Board: Blasting Off to Good Health!

Materials

rocket flame pattern (page 9)
star pattern (page 9)
orange and yellow
   construction paper

dark blue craft paper
pipe cleaners
cardboard tubes
tempera paints

snow cone cups
glitter (optional)
paintbrushes

border
glue
pencil

tape
stapler
scissors

Teacher Directions

1. Prepare a bulletin board with dark blue paper. Add the border and title "Blasting Off to Good Health!"
2. Trace several stars on yellow paper and cut them out. (You may wish to have children glue glitter on the stars.)
3. Cut pipe cleaners in half and wrap them around a pencil to make a spring. Tape one end of a pipe cleaner spring to the back of each star. Staple the free end of each spring to the board. The stars will not touch the board, and their movement will make them look like they are "sparkling."
4. Trace a rocket flame on orange paper for each child. Cut out the flames.
5. Write each child's good health practice on a rocket flame before it is glued inside the tube.
6. Staple the completed rockets to the board.

Student Directions

1. Paint a tube to make the body of the rocket. Set it aside to dry.
2. Paint a snow cone cup to make the cone of the rocket. Set it aside to dry.
3. Write your name on the rocket body.
4. Glue the nose cone on one end of the rocket.
5. Get a rocket flame. Think of a good health practice. Ask someone to write the health practice on the flame.
6. Glue the flame to the other end of the tube.

Health, Nutrition, and P.E. PreK–K, SV 141902356X

Rocket Flame and Star Patterns

rocket flame

star

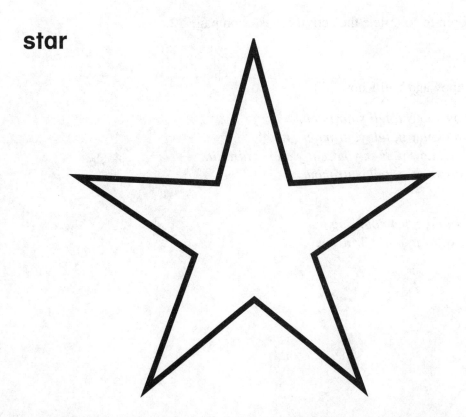

Health, Nutrition, and P.E. PreK–K, SV 141902356X

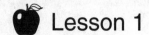 **Lesson 1**

Feelings

Standards

- Identifies and practices personal health habits that help individuals stay healthy
- Demonstrates how to seek the help of parents/guardians and other trusted adults in making decisions and solving problems
- Recognizes and describes individual differences and communicates appropriately with all individuals

You Need

- feelings face cards (page 11)

Do This

1. Duplicate the face cards so that each child gets one. Have children take turns holding up their card to identify the feeling. Ask them to mimic the face and tell a time they felt that way.

2. Tell children that some feelings can make them feel uncomfortable, and they can do things to change these feelings, such as ride a bike when they are mad or pet a dog when they are sad.

3. Teach children the "Feelings Change" song at the bottom of the page. Invite them to make up other verses.

Optional: Invite children to complete the activity master on page 12.

Feelings Change

(Sung to "If You're Happy and You Know It")

If you're scared and you know it, tell your mom.
If you're scared and you know it, tell your mom.
If you're scared and you know it, then you really can control it.
If you're scared and you know it, tell your mom.

Other verses:
If you're sad and you know it, pet your dog.
If you're mad and you know it, paint or draw.

Health, Nutrition, and P.E. PreK–K, SV 141902356X

Feelings Face Cards

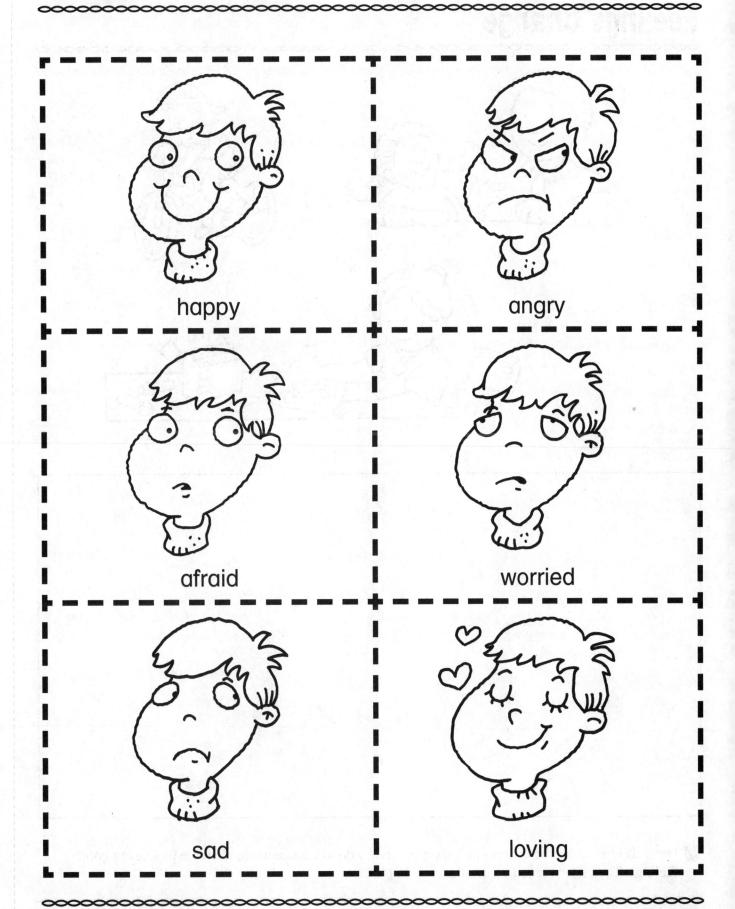

happy

angry

afraid

worried

sad

loving

Health, Nutrition, and P.E. PreK–K, SV 141902356X

Feelings Change

🍎 Have children color the pictures that show what they do to change uncomfortable feelings to good feelings. Then have them draw another way in the box.

Health, Nutrition, and P.E. PreK–K, SV 141902356X

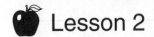 Lesson 2

Me on the Outside

Standards

• Names major body parts and their functions

Do This

1. Take children to a large area where there is plenty of wall space. Have them find their own personal space along the wall.

2. Name different body parts that children touch against the wall. Name as many different parts as possible.

3. Gather children. Name each body part again and ask children to point to it. Then, discuss what each part does.

4. Teach children the "Move Your Body" song at the bottom of the page. Invite them to make up other verses.

Optional: Invite children to complete the activity master on page 14.

Move Your Body

(Sung to "Row, Row, Row Your Boat")

Nod, nod, nod your head.
Feel it move around.
Move it left and move it right.
Move it up and down.

Swing, swing, swing your arms.
Feel them move around.
Move them left and move them right.
Move them up and down.

Other verses:
Stretch, stretch, stretch your trunk.
Bend, bend, bend your legs.

Health, Nutrition, and P.E. PreK–K, SV 141902356X

Name _____ Date _____

Me on the Outside

head
_____

- - - - - - - - - - - - - -
_____

arms
_____

- - - - - - - - - - - - - -
_____

trunk
_____

trunk

legs
_____

- - - - - - - - - - - - - -
_____

🍎 Help children read the words. Then, have them write each word and draw a line from the word to the matching body part.

www.harcourtschoolsupply.com
© Harcourt Achieve Inc. All rights reserved.

14

Unit 1: Health
Health, Nutrition, and P.E. PreK–K, SV 141902356X

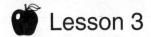 Lesson 3

Me on the Inside

Standards

• Names major body parts and their functions

You Need

• stethoscope
• paper cups
• scissors

Do This

1. Display a stethoscope and identify it. Have children tell where they might see a stethoscope. Tell how it is used.

2. Distribute a paper cup to each child. Help children cut out the bottom of the cup. Explain that it is like a stethoscope and will help them hear parts inside the body move.

3. Invite partners to take turns holding the larger end of the cup gently against the back. Challenge them to listen for the heartbeat.

4. Next, have partners listen to stomach and lung sounds.

5. Gather children and identify the body parts they heard. Identify the function of each part.

6. Point out the brain and its main function of thinking.

7. Point out that bones let the body stand and move, and they also protect soft organs.

8. Teach children the "Inside of Me" poem at the bottom of the page. Invite them to point to each part when it is mentioned.

Optional: Invite children to complete the activity master on page 16.

Inside of Me

Inside of me are many things,
And I can say them all.
A brain that thinks,
A heart that beats,
Two lungs that breathe,
A stomach to eat,
A spine in a line,
Blood that's red,
And lots of bones from my toes to my head.

Health, Nutrition, and P.E. PreK–K, SV 141902356X

Me on the Inside

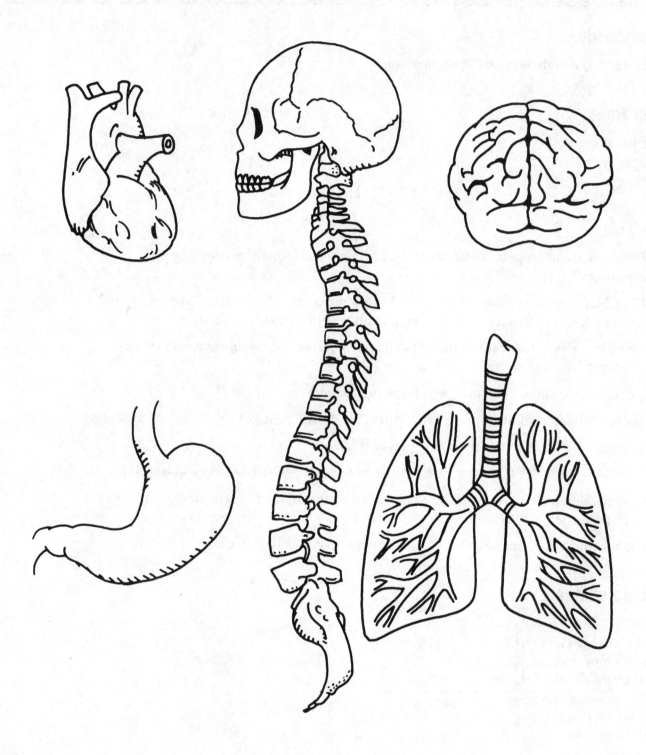

🍎 Have children color the heart red, the lungs blue, the brain green, the stomach orange, and the skull and spine yellow.

Health, Nutrition, and P.E. PreK–K, SV 141902356X

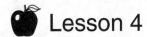 Lesson 4

Bones

Standards

• Names major body parts and their functions

You Need

• rag doll
• X-rays
• skeleton bones patterns (pages 18 and 19)

Do This

1. Enlarge and duplicate a set of the skeleton bones patterns. Cut them apart and laminate them if possible.

2. Ask children to feel body parts where bones are easily felt, such as wrists, knees, or fingers.

3. Display a rag doll and try to make it stand and move. Then have children stand. Guide them to understand that bones help people stand and move.

4. Ask children to feel their head and rib cage. Point out that bones help keep body parts safe.

5. Show children an X-ray. Identify the bone and where it is in the body.

6. Display the different bones and show where they are in the body. Pass the parts out to individual children.

7. Teach children the "Bones Make Up the Skeleton" song at the bottom of the page. Invite children having those parts to come forward and put the skeleton together, like a puzzle.

Optional: Invite children to complete the activity master on page 20.

Bones Make Up the Skeleton

(Sung to "Skip to My Lou")

In my body, I have a skull.
In my body, I have a skull.
In my body, I have a skull.
My bones make up my skeleton.

Other verses:
In my body, I have spine bones.
In my body, I have some ribs.
In my body, I have arm bones.
In my body, I have a hipbone.
In my body, I have leg bones.

Health, Nutrition, and P.E. PreK–K, SV 141902356X

Skeleton Bones Patterns

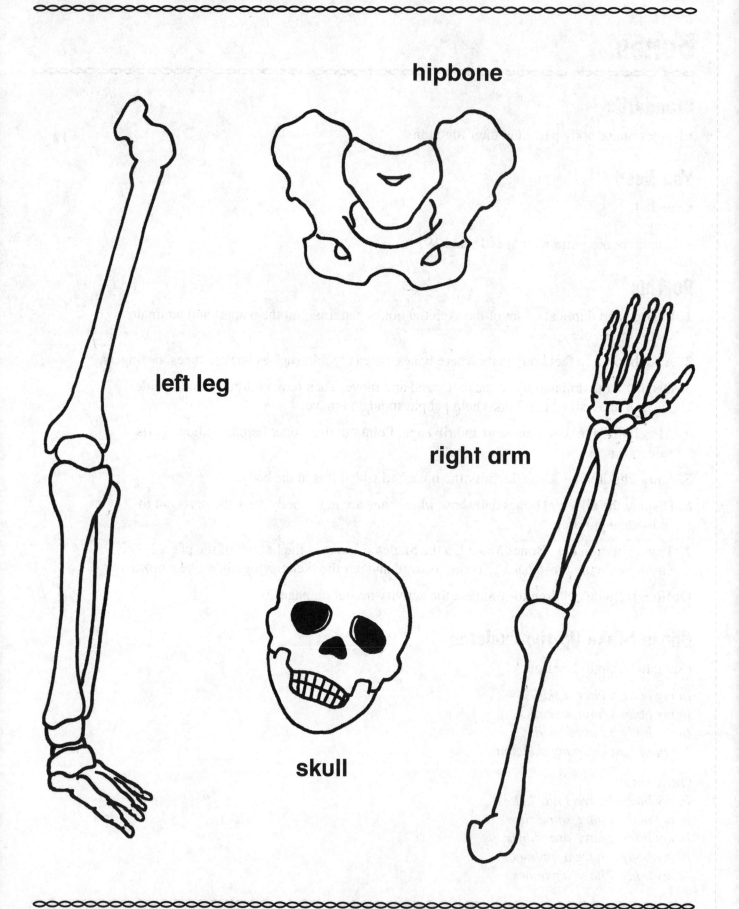

hipbone

left leg

right arm

skull

Health, Nutrition, and P.E. PreK–K, SV 141902356X

Skeleton Bones Patterns

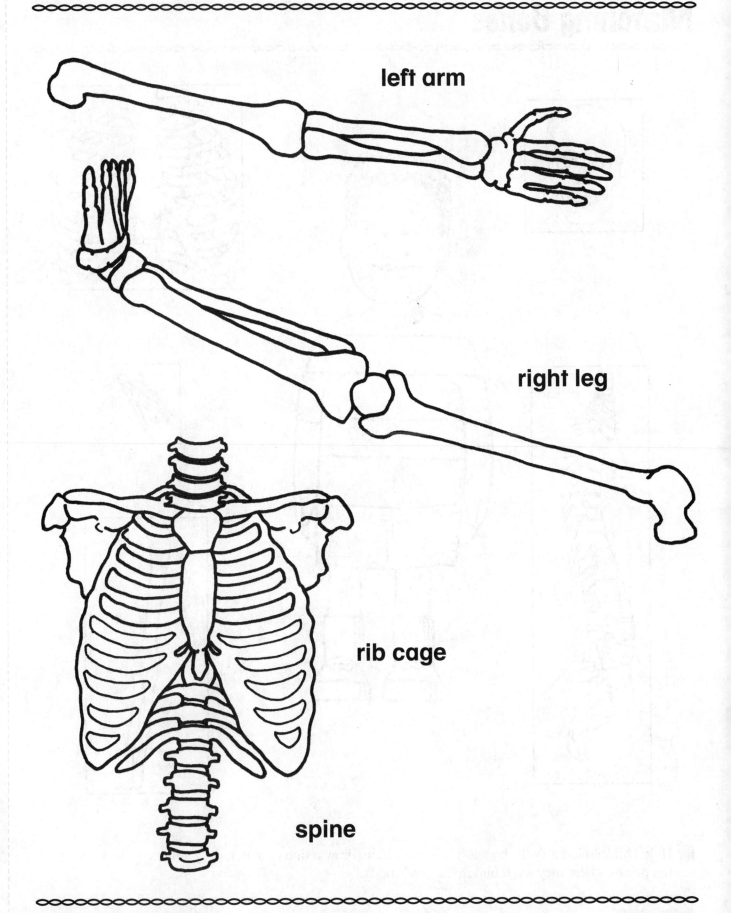

left arm

right leg

rib cage

spine

Health, Nutrition, and P.E. PreK–K, SV 141902356X

Matching Bones

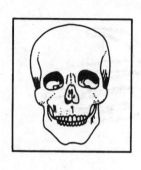

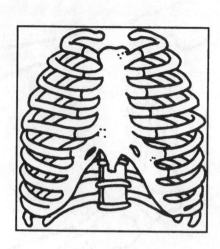

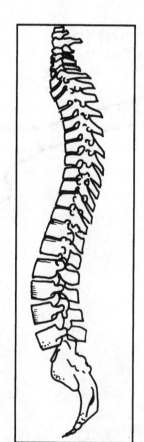

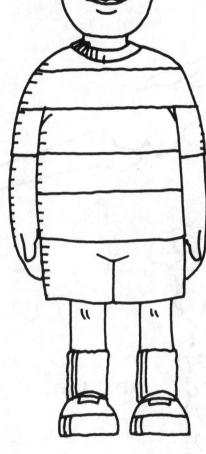

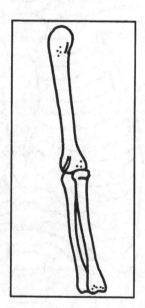

🍎 Help children identify the bones. Then, have them draw a line to match the pictures of the bones to the places where they are found in the boy's body.

   Health, Nutrition, and P.E. PreK–K, SV 141902356X

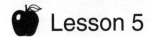 Lesson 5

The Brain

Standards

- Identifies and practices personal health habits that help individuals stay healthy
- Identifies the purpose of protective equipment
- Names major body parts and their functions

You Need

- a resource book showing a simple diagram of the brain

Do This

1. Have children identify where their brain is located. Explain that the brain is inside the skull. Compare the skull to a bike helmet in that both keep the brain from being hurt.

2. Display a simple diagram of the brain. Explain that the brain controls how the body works.

3. Teach children the "My Brain Helps Me" song at the bottom of the page. Ask them to listen for the activities that the brain controls.

4. Explain that it is important to keep the brain healthy. Share the following behaviors children should do.
    - Eat good, nutritious food.
    - Get plenty of sleep.
    - Read books and ask questions to learn things.
    - Wear a helmet when bike riding or skating to keep the brain from getting hurt.

Optional: Invite children to complete the activity master on page 22.

My Brain Helps Me

(Sung to "The Farmer in the Dell")

My brain helps me walk.
My brain helps me walk.
My brain controls my body,
So my brain helps me walk.

Other verses:
My brain helps me talk.
My brain helps me think.
My brain helps me feel.

Health, Nutrition, and P.E. PreK–K, SV 141902356X

A Healthy Brain

1.

2.

3.

4.

Have children color the picture in each row that shows the better way to keep the brain healthy.

Health, Nutrition, and P.E. PreK–K, SV 141902356X

Name _____ Date _____

Kelly Is Special

Kelly is special. No one looks like Kelly.
No one does what Kelly can do.

1

---- Fold ----

Activity

How are you special? Draw a picture.

Have someone help you write about
the picture.

_____

_____

_____

4

Kelly has many different feelings.

Sometimes Kelly gets angry. She talks to her mom about her feelings. She gets help to feel better.

2

Kelly is good at jumping rope. Jumping rope helps Kelly's body grow strong.

Kelly likes to play games, too. Games help Kelly's brain grow strong.

3

Health, Nutrition, and P.E. PreK–K, SV 141902356X

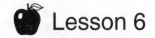 Lesson 6

The Five Senses

Standards

• Names the five senses
• Names major body parts and their functions

You Need

• sense body parts patterns (pages 26 and 27)
• paper bags
• construction paper
• glue
• scissors

Do This

1. Duplicate a set of sense body parts for each child. Cut them out.

2. Explain that there are five parts of the body that help them learn about the things in their world. Name the senses and the corresponding body parts.

3. Teach children the "Our Five Senses" song at the bottom of the page.

4. Invite children to make a five senses puppet. Have them gather the body parts, color them, and glue them on the bag.

Optional: Invite children to complete the activity master on page 28.

Our Five Senses

(Sung to "Are You Sleeping?")

Our five senses, our five senses—
We use them all, we use them all.
Seeing, hearing, touching,
Smelling, and tasting.
There are five, there are five.

I use my ears, I use my ears
To hear many things, to hear many things.
Bells, horns, and drums,
Singing and talking.
Ears can hear, ears can hear.

I use my eyes, I use my eyes
To see many things, to see many things.
Rainbows, books, and stars,
Butterflies and baseballs.
Eyes can see, eyes can see.

I use my nose, I use my nose
To smell many things, to smell many things.
Roses, soap, and bread,
Garbage cans and skunks.
Noses can smell, noses can smell.

I use my tongue, I use my tongue
To taste many things, to taste many things.
Ice cream, apples, oranges,
Pickles, and popcorn.
Tongues can taste, tongues can taste.

I use my fingers, I use my fingers
To touch many things, to touch many things.
Bunnies, ice, and rocks,
Cactus and sandpaper.
Fingers can touch, fingers can touch.

Sense Body Parts Patterns

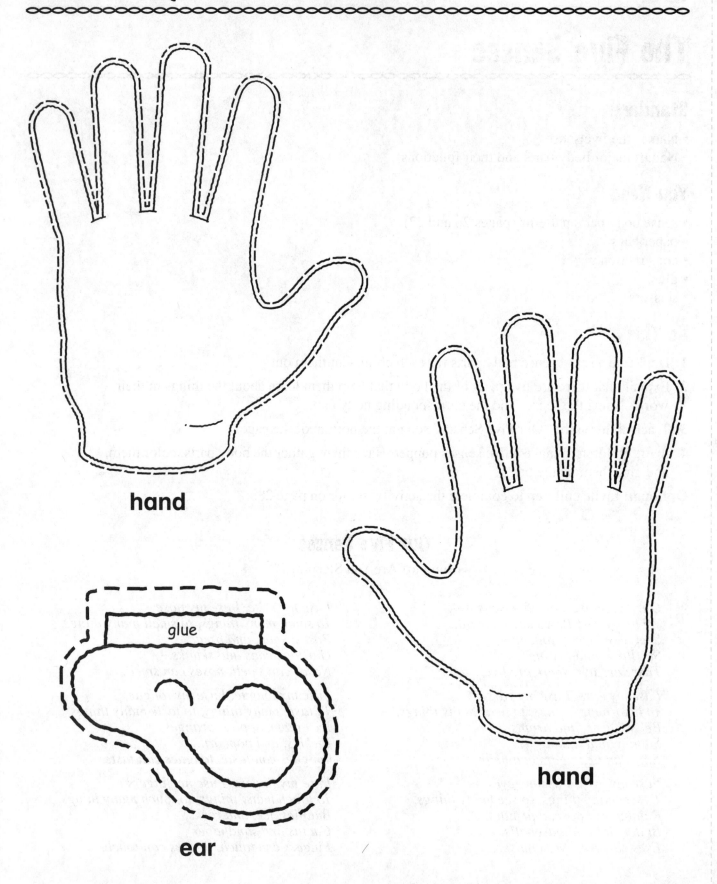

hand

hand

glue

ear

Health, Nutrition, and P.E. PreK–K, SV 141902356X

Sense Body Parts Patterns

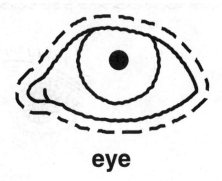

eye

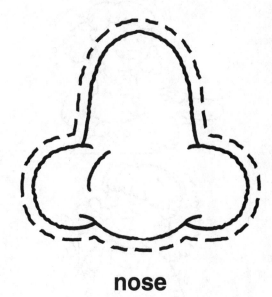

nose

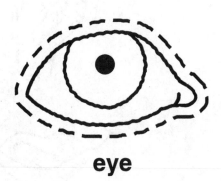

eye

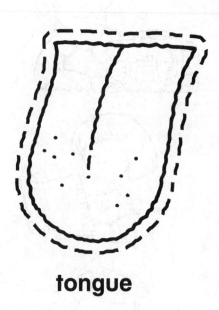

tongue

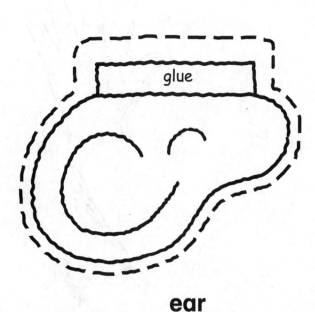

glue

ear

Health, Nutrition, and P.E. PreK–K, SV 141902356X

The Five Senses

1.

2.

3.

4.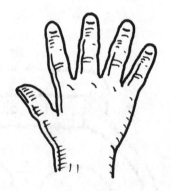

5.

🍎 Have children draw a line from each picture to the body part they would most likely use.

Health, Nutrition, and P.E. PreK–K, SV 141902356X

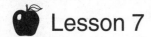 Lesson 7

Your Eyes

Standards

- Identifies and practices personal health habits that help individuals stay healthy
- Names the five senses
- Names major body parts and their functions
- Names and identifies people who can provide helpful information

You Need

- *Brown Bear, Brown Bear, What Do You See?* by Bill Martin, Jr. (HarperCollins)
- small balls

Do This

1. Read aloud *Brown Bear, Brown Bear, What Do You See?* Discuss how the eyes help animals see.

2. Using the patterned text of *Brown Bear, Brown Bear, What Do You See?*, ask each child what he or she sees. (Example: *Juan, Juan, what do you see?*)

3. Ask children if two eyes are better than one. Then, assign partners and invite them to do an experiment.
   - Partners stand five feet apart.
   - They toss a ball to each other ten times.
   - Partners close one eye and toss the ball ten more times.

4. Discuss the results of the experiment.

5. Ask *Are two eyes better than one?*

6. Teach children the "Eye Care" poem at the bottom of the page. Discuss other ways to keep the eyes safe, such as visiting an eye doctor for a checkup.

Optional: Invite children to complete the activity master on page 30.

Eye Care

We need our eyes.
They help us see.
So follow these rules
For their safety.
Wear dark glasses
When you're in the sun.
And use a light
For reading fun.
Put on goggles
When using tools.
We need our eyes,
So follow these rules.

Eye Care

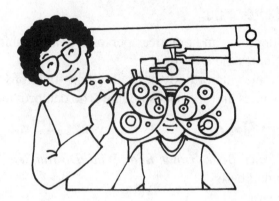

🍎 Have children cross out the pictures that show poor eye care.

Health, Nutrition, and P.E. PreK–K, SV 141902356X

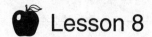 Lesson 8

Your Nose

Standards

- Names the five senses
- Names major body parts and their functions

You Need

- 8 containers with lids
- cotton balls
- flavored extracts (lemon, almond, peppermint, clear vanilla)

Do This

1. Put a few drops of each extract on two cotton balls. Put the scented balls in separate containers.

2. Put the containers in a center. Invite children to match the two containers that are the same.

3. At the end of the day, gather children. Invite them to identify the different scents.

4. Teach children the "Rose or Toes" poem at the bottom of the page.

Optional: Invite children to complete the activity master on page 32.

Rose or Toes

When I smell, I use my nose.
It helps me sniff a lovely rose.
But sometimes with my stinky toes
I use my fingers to keep it closed.

Name _____ Date _____

Use Your Nose

1. _____ smells sweet.

2. _____ smells spicy.

3. _____ smells fresh.

4. _____ smells sour.

🍎 Have children dictate or write words to complete the sentences.
Then, have them draw a picture of each item.

Health, Nutrition, and P.E. PreK–K, SV 141902356X

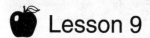 **Lesson 9**

Your Hands

Standards

• Names the five senses
• Names major body parts and their functions

You Need

• five textured items (sandpaper, cotton, aluminum foil, fuzzy material, lace, etc.)
• construction paper
• marker
• scissors
• glue

Do This

1. Cut the five items into one-inch squares. Cut enough for each child to have a set.

2. Lead children in a discussion of the sense of touch.

3. Have children gather one of each textured square.

4. Say words that describe the textures and have children hold up the corresponding square.

5. Help children trace one hand on construction paper.

6. Invite them to glue each square to a fingertip.

7. Have them write or dictate a sentence telling one thing they like to touch. Record the sentence on the center of the hand.

8. Teach children the "My Pillow" poem at the bottom of the page.

Optional: Invite children to complete the activity master on page 34.

My Pillow

My hand can touch a cat that's fluffy
Or a tire that is bumpy.
But my pillow puzzles me—
It's fluffy, and it's lumpy!

Health, Nutrition, and P.E. PreK–K, SV 141902356X

Name _____ Date _____

How Does It Feel?

🍎 Help children identify the pictures. Then, tell them to look at the first picture in each row. Have them draw a circle around the picture in the row that would feel the same.

Unit 1: Health
Health, Nutrition, and P.E. PreK–K, SV 141902356X

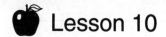 **Lesson 10**

Your Ears

Standards

• Identifies and practices personal health habits that help individuals stay healthy
• Names the five senses
• Names major body parts and their functions
• Names and identifies people who can provide helpful information

You Need

• four items that make noise (bell, drum, pencil sharpener, whistle, etc.)
• pencils

Do This

1. Invite children to put their head down and close their eyes. Use the items to make noises for the children to identify.

2. Discuss the sense of hearing.

3. Ask children if two ears are better than one. Then, assign partners and invite them to do an experiment.
   • One child sits in a chair. The partner stands anywhere behind this child and taps two pencils.
   • The seated child tells from which direction the tapping is coming. Encourage the standing partner to move around four times.
   • Next, the seated child covers one ear while the standing partner taps the pencils.
   • Children reverse roles.

4. Discuss the results of the experiment.

5. Ask *Are two ears better than one?*

6. Teach children the "Ear Care" poem at the bottom of the page. Discuss other ways to keep the ears safe, such as not poking objects inside.

Optional: Invite children to complete the activity master on page 36.

Ear Care

I wash my ears when I bathe.
I turn the TV down.
I visit the doctor for a hearing checkup,
So now I can hear every sound.

Name _____   Date _____

Take Care of Your Ears

🍎 Have children color the pictures that show good ear care.

Health, Nutrition, and P.E. PreK–K, SV 141902356X

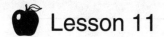 **Lesson 11**

Your Tongue

Standards

- Names the five senses
- Names major body parts and their functions

You Need

- mirror
- salted popcorn
- sour pickles
- mini-marshmallows
- unsweetened chocolate baking squares
- paper plates
- knife
- paper cups
- water

Do This

1. Cut the pickles and chocolate into small bites.

2. Discuss the sense of taste. Invite children to look in a mirror to see the bumps on their tongue. Explain that those bumps are taste buds that help them taste four flavors: salty, sour, bitter, and sweet.

3. Put a small amount of the four foods on a plate for each child. Pour water into the cups. Pass out a plate and water cup to each child.

4. Invite children to taste each food and decide if it is salty, sour, bitter, or sweet. Tell them to take a drink of water to rinse the taste from the tongue between each food.

5. Discuss the results of the experiment.

6. Teach children the "Tongue Tastes" poem at the bottom of the page.

Optional: Invite children to complete the activity master on page 38.

Tongue Tastes

My tongue is bumpy, but I don't care.
Those bumps help me to taste.
Salty, sour, bitter, or sweet—
My tongue tells me what's great.

Unit 1: Health
Health, Nutrition, and P.E. PreK–K, SV 141902356X

Name _____ Date _____

Tasting Food

| salty | sour | sweet | bitter |

I.

_____

- -

_____

2.

_____

- -

_____

3.

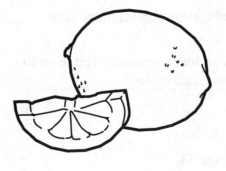

_____

- -

_____

4.

_____

- -

_____

🍎 Have children write a word from the box to identify each food taste.

Health, Nutrition, and P.E. PreK–K, SV 141902356X

Name _____

Date _____

Jerry's Five Senses

Jerry has five senses.
He uses them every day.

1

Fold

Activity

How do you use your senses?
Draw a picture.

Have someone help you write the
names of the senses you used.

_____

_____

4

Unit 1: Health
Health, Nutrition, and P.E. PreK–K, SV 141902356X

Jerry talks on the phone. He uses his ears to hear what his friends say.

Jerry pets and hugs his dog. He uses his hands to touch the fluffy fur.

2

Jerry eats breakfast. He uses his nose to smell the food. He uses his tongue to taste the food.

Jerry walks across the street safely. He uses his eyes to look for signs and cars.

3

Health, Nutrition, and P.E. PreK–K, SV 141902356X

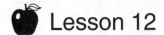 Lesson 12

Your Teeth

Standards

• Names major body parts and their functions

You Need

• tooth puppet patterns (page 42)
• small paper plates
• tempera paint
• white, black, tan, and pink construction paper
• mini-marshmallows
• mirror
• paintbrushes
• paint containers
• glue
• scissors

Do This

1. Duplicate, trace, and cut out the following puppet pieces for each child: two white eyes, two black pupils, one tan nose, and one pink tongue.

2. Invite each child to make a tooth puppet.
   • Fold a plate in half.
   • Paint the inside of the plate red.
   • Glue the eyes and nose on one side of the plate.
   • Glue the tongue on the inside of the plate.
   • Glue the marshmallows along the inside top and bottom of the plate for teeth.
   • Set the plate aside to dry.

3. Have children look in a mirror. Discuss the parts of a tooth (crown and root) and the gum that hides the root.

4. Point out the three kinds of teeth (biting, tearing, and chewing) and their uses.

5. Explore the topic of baby and adult teeth. Invite children to discuss the baby teeth they have lost.

6. Teach children the "Baby Teeth" poem at the bottom of the page.

Optional: Invite children to complete the activity master on page 43.

Baby Teeth

Baby teeth are meant to fall out on their own.
Adult teeth will come in and last until you're grown.
Be sure to take good care—they're the only teeth you've got.
Brush and floss every day so your teeth will never rot.

Tooth Puppet Patterns

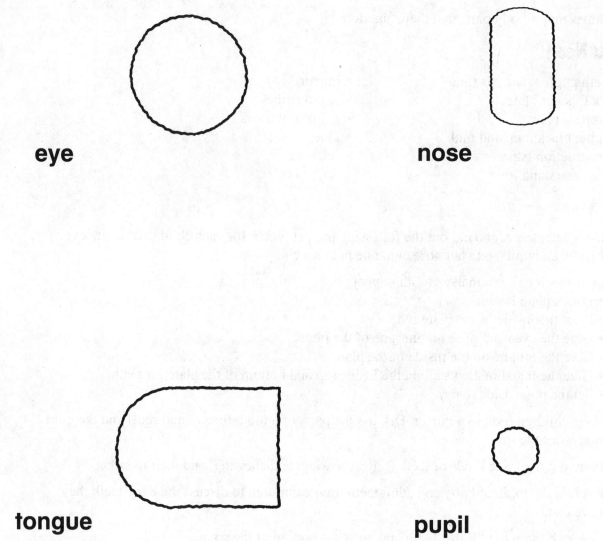

eye

nose

tongue

pupil

Health, Nutrition, and P.E. PreK–K, SV 141902356X

Your Tooth

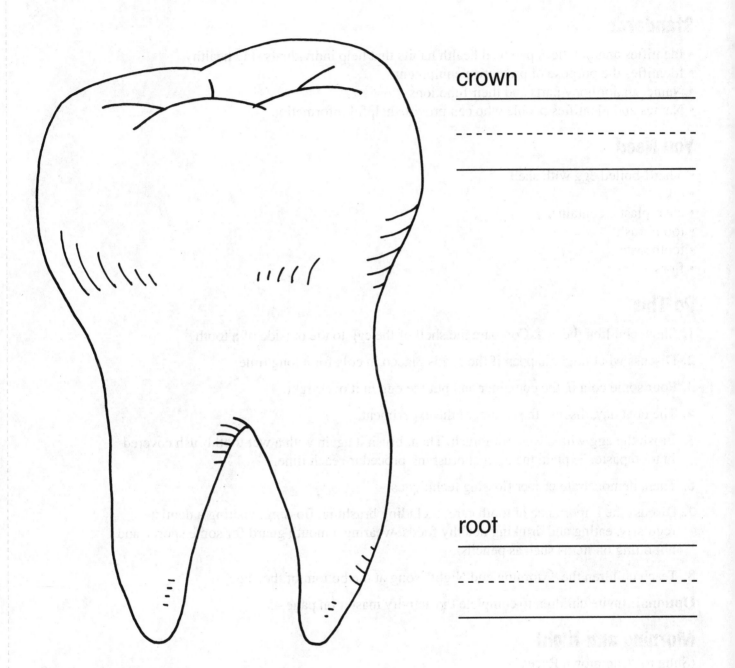

crown
_____
- -
_____

root
_____
- -
_____

🍎 Help children read the words. Then, have them write each word and draw a line from the word to the matching tooth part. Finally, give them a sheet of pink paper. Tell them it represents the gum. Have them make a glue line along one edge and place it on the tooth to cover the root.

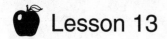 Lesson 13

Caring for Your Teeth

Standards

- Identifies and practices personal health habits that help individuals stay healthy
- Identifies the purpose of protective equipment
- Names major body parts and their functions
- Names and identifies people who can provide helpful information

You Need

- a hard-boiled egg with shell
- cola
- clear plastic container
- toothbrush
- toothpaste
- floss

Do This

1. Show children the egg. Compare the shell of the egg to the outside of a tooth.

2. Discuss what might happen if the egg is placed in cola for a long time.

3. Pour some cola in the container and put the egg in it overnight.

4. The next day, discuss the results of the experiment.

5. Brush the egg with a wet toothbrush. Then, brush it again with a wet toothbrush covered in toothpaste. Explain the correct brushing procedure each time.

6. Then, demonstrate proper flossing techniques.

7. Discuss the importance of tooth care, including brushing, flossing, visiting a dentist regularly, eating and drinking healthy foods, wearing a mouth guard for some sports, and not biting on items such as pencils.

8. Teach children the "Morning and Night" song at the bottom of the page.

Optional: Invite children to complete the activity master on page 45.

Morning and Night

(Sung to "Camptown Races")

Brush your teeth two times a day—morning and night.
Doing this will help keep cavities away.
Use a soft toothbrush.
Brush slowly, don't you rush.
Brush and floss to keep teeth strong.
Teeth will last your whole life long.

Name _____ Date _____

Be Careful with Your Teeth

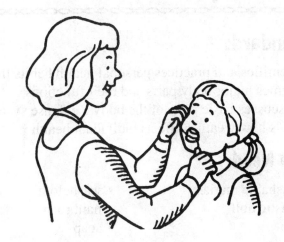

🍎 Have children color the pictures that show children taking good care of their teeth.

Health, Nutrition, and P.E. PreK–K, SV 141902356X

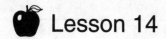 Lesson 14

Healthy Skin

Standards

- Identifies and practices personal health habits that help individuals stay healthy
- Names major body parts and their functions
- Discusses basic parts of the body's defense system against germs
- Tells how weather affects individual health

You Need

- washable marker
- plastic doll
- tub
- water
- washcloth
- nailbrush
- soap
- sunscreen

Do This

1. Use the washable marker to draw several spots on the doll to represent dirt. Include spots on the fingernails.

2. Discuss how the skin keeps the inside of the body safe. Compare the skin to a food wrapper.

3. Put the doll in a tub of water. Point out that water alone does not remove the marker. Repeat the demonstration using a cloth, soap, and a nailbrush.

4. Discuss why it is important to use soap, a washcloth, and a nailbrush to clean the skin, hair, and nails. Explain that these tools keep the body healthy.

5. Next, put the doll in bright sunlight. Discuss how the bright, hot sun can hurt the skin.

6. Put sunscreen on the doll and explain the purpose of the lotion.

7. Teach children the "Keep Our Skin Healthy" song at the bottom of the page.

Optional: Invite children to complete the activity master on page 47.

Keep Our Skin Healthy

(Sung to "Here We Go 'Round the Mulberry Bush")

This is the way we wash our hands,
Wash our hands, wash our hands.
This is the way we wash our hands,
To keep our skin healthy.

Other verses:
This is the way we clean our nails.
This is the way we wash our hair.
This is the way we put sunscreen on.

Name _____ Date _____

Be Careful with Your Skin

🍎 Have children color the pictures that show children taking good care of their skin.

Health, Nutrition, and P.E. PreK–K, SV 141902356X

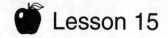 **Lesson 15**

Germs

Standards

- Identifies and practices personal health habits that help individuals stay healthy
- Explains practices used to control the spread of germs
- Discusses basic parts of the body's defense system against germs

You Need

- hand pattern (page 49)
- paper plate
- white construction paper
- spray bottle
- food color
- water
- tissues
- marker
- scissors
- glue

Do This

1. Duplicate a hand pattern on white construction paper for each child.

2. Draw a face on a paper plate. Cut out a hole for the nose and mouth.

3. Fill a spray bottle with water and several drops of food color.

4. Have children hold one of their hands close to their face and cough. Then, have them exhale heavily as if sneezing. Point out that they feel air and moisture coming from their mouth and nose.

5. Position the spray bottle behind the mouth of the paper plate face. Make a coughing sound and spray the water on a hand pattern. Repeat to exhibit sneezing.

6. Explain that there are germs in the air and liquid coming from the mouth and nose. Then, discuss germs and how they are spread.

7. Teach children the "Keep Germs Away" poem at the bottom of the page. Ask them to listen for ways to keep germs from spreading.

8. Allow children to spray the hand pattern with the colored water and glue a tissue to the page. Invite them to write or dictate a sentence about germs.

Optional: Invite children to complete the activity master on page 50.

Keep Germs Away

Germs are small.
They're hard to see.
When I'm sick,
They're all on me.
To stay safe,
Here's what I'll do
So I'll keep germs
Away from you!

I'll use my hand
To cover a cough.
I'll sneeze in tissues
To keep germs off.
There's one more thing
For me to do.
I'll wash my hands
When I am through!

Health, Nutrition, and P.E. PreK–K, SV 141902356X

Hand Pattern

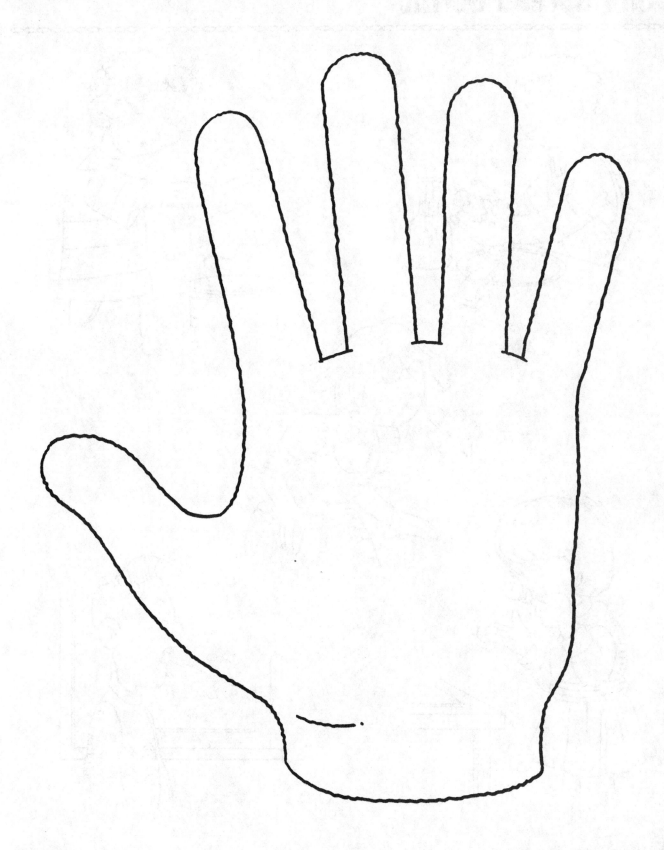

Name _____ Date _____

Don't Spread Germs

🍎 Have children cross out the pictures that show germs being spread.

Health, Nutrition, and P.E. PreK–K, SV 141902356X

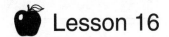 **Lesson 16**

Stress

Standards

- Identifies and practices personal health habits that help individuals stay healthy
- Demonstrates how to seek the help of parents/guardians and other trusted adults in making decisions

You Need

- stress level chart (page 52)
- white construction paper
- crayons
- tape
- scissors

Do This

1. Make a sample stress level chart.
   - Color the pictures and cut slits along the dotted lines.
   - Cut apart the three strips. Color one strip red.
   - Tape the three strips together with the red strip in the middle.
   - Insert one end of the strip through the bottom slit. Pull it through to the front and insert it into the top slit.

2. Duplicate a stress chart on white paper for each child.

3. Discuss stress. Include examples of stressful situations and how to recognize the feelings.

4. Display the stress chart and point out the pictures. Have children explain how they can tell the child is getting more and more stressed. Move the slide so the red aligns with each picture to show that the feelings of stress are increasing.

5. Teach children the "If You're Feeling Too Much Stress" song at the bottom of the page. Invite them to listen for ways to reduce stress. Encourage them to create new verses to tell how they would get rid of stress.

6. Invite children to make their own stress chart.

Optional: Invite children to complete the activity master on page 53.

If You're Feeling Too Much Stress

(Sung to "If You're Happy and You Know It")

If you're feeling too much stress, read a book.
If you're feeling too much stress, read a book.
If you're feeling too much stress, then your face and body show it.
If you're feeling too much stress, read a book.

Other verses:
If you're feeling too much stress, have a talk.
If you're feeling too much stress, take a walk.

Health, Nutrition, and P.E. PreK–K, SV 141902356X

Name _____ Date _____

Stress Level Chart

.... cut line ....

.... cut line ....

Unit 1: Health
Health, Nutrition, and P.E. PreK–K, SV 141902356X

Name _____   Date _____

Get Rid of Stress

🍎 Have children color pictures that show how they would handle stress. Then, have them draw and color one more way in the box.

Health, Nutrition, and P.E. PreK–K, SV 141902356X

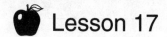 Lesson 17

Medicines

Standards

- Identifies and practices personal health habits that help individuals stay healthy
- Identifies ways to avoid harming oneself or another person
- Identifies and uses refusal skills to avoid unsafe behavior situations

You Need

- safe medicine picture cards (page 55)
- pictures of over-the-counter (OTC) medicines cut out from magazines (lotions, pills, liquids)
- magazines
- empty prescription bottle with your name
- chart paper
- white construction paper
- markers
- glue
- scissors

Do This

1. Enlarge and duplicate the picture cards. Color and cut them apart.

2. Glue the OTC medicine pictures to chart paper.

3. Display the chart and talk about the medicines in the pictures. Discuss where medicines come from and what they are used for.

4. Invite children to find and cut out a picture of other OTC medicines to glue to the chart.

5. Next, show children the prescription bottle. Discuss where people get prescriptions filled and why.

6. Point out your name on the label. Explain that no one except you can take the prescription. Have children practice refusal skills.

7. Display each picture card. Discuss who is giving prescription medicine in each picture and if children should take the pills.

8. Teach children the "Prescriptions" poem at the bottom of the page.

Optional: Invite children to complete the activity master on page 56.

Prescriptions

Sometimes when you are feeling ill,
A doctor will give you some pills.
Read the label. Look for your name.
Everyone else will do the same.
Get the pills from an adult you know.
Soon you'll be better and on the go.

Safe Medicine Picture Cards

Health, Nutrition, and P.E. PreK–K, SV 141902356X

Name _____ Date _____

My Medicine

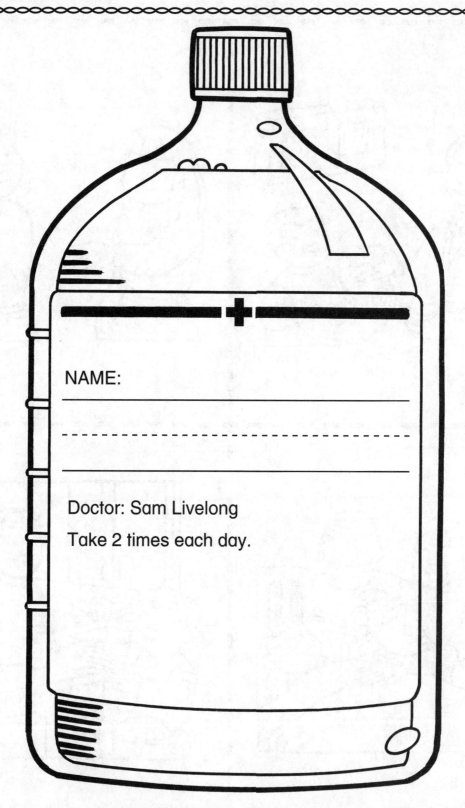

NAME:

_____

- -

_____

Doctor: Sam Livelong

Take 2 times each day.

🍎 Remind children to take medicine only from a trusted adult and from a bottle with their name. Have children write their name on the label and color the bottle.

    Health, Nutrition, and P.E. PreK–K, SV 141902356X

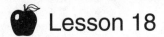 **Lesson 18**

Fire Safety

Standards

- Identifies and practices personal health habits that help individuals stay healthy
- Identifies ways to avoid harming oneself or another person
- Demonstrates procedures for responding to emergencies
- Recognizes and explains the importance of manners and rules for healthy communication

You Need

- stop, drop, and roll picture cards (page 58)
- telephone
- pictures of things with flames
- chart paper
- red construction paper
- double-stick tape
- glue
- scissors

Do This

1. Enlarge and duplicate the stop, drop, and roll picture cards. Color and cut the pictures apart. Glue them in order on chart paper.

2. Cut several flame shapes out of red paper. Add double-stick tape backings.

3. Display pictures of things with flames. Discuss how fires can start (matches, lighters, candles, stoves, and fireworks) and fire safety.

4. Explain that clothes can sometimes catch on fire. Show the stop, drop, and roll picture cards. Point out each step and have children practice the movements.

5. Move to a large, indoor area to play flame tag. Give the flame cutouts with tape backings to several children. They will be "taggers." The taggers stick the flames to others. Children must stop, drop, and roll when tagged. Then they become the taggers.

6. Gather children and discuss the emergency phone number 911. Have them role-play dialing 911 on a phone, saying their name, and stating there is a fire emergency.

7. Teach children the "Stop, Drop, and Roll" poem at the bottom of the page.

Optional: Invite children to complete the activity master on page 59.

Stop, Drop, and Roll

If my clothes catch on fire,
I know just what to do.
I S-T-O-P, stop.
I D-R-O-P, drop.
I R-O-L-L, roll.
That's just what I will do!

Health, Nutrition, and P.E. PreK–K, SV 141902356X

Stop, Drop, and Roll Picture Cards

Health, Nutrition, and P.E. PreK–K, SV 141902356X

Call for Help

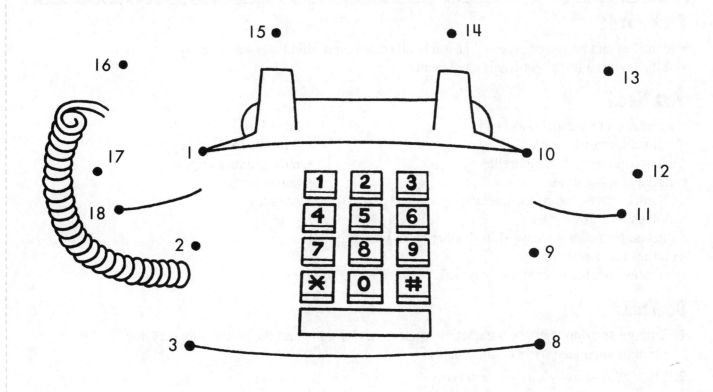

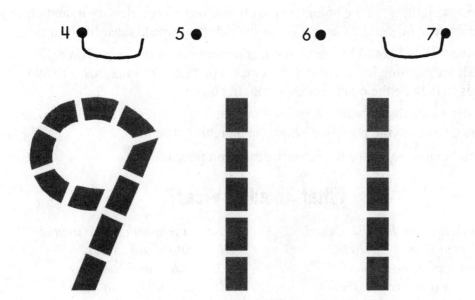

🍎 Have children connect the dots to make the telephone and then trace the 911 numbers.

Health, Nutrition, and P.E. PreK–K, SV 141902356X

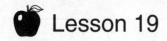 **Lesson 19**

Weather Wear

Standards

• Identifies and practices personal health habits that help individuals stay healthy
• Tells how weather affects individual health

You Need

• weather picture cards (page 61)
• clothes for rainy weather
  (raincoat, rain boots, umbrella)
• clothes for hot weather
  (T-shirt, shorts, swimsuit, sandals)
• clothes for fall weather
  (jacket, pants, long-sleeve shirt, leather shoes)
• clothes for winter weather
  (mittens, hat, heavy coat, snow boots)

• large box
• 4 pieces of chart paper
• recycled magazines
• markers
• scissors
• glue

Do This

1. Enlarge and duplicate the weather picture cards. Color and cut the pictures apart. Glue them on separate pieces of chart paper.

2. Place all of the clothing inside a box.

3. Display the four pictures. Discuss the weather shown in each and the time of year children would experience it.

4. Point out the box of clothing. Invite volunteers to choose one piece, identify it, and place it in front of the picture showing the weather during which they would most likely wear it.

5. Teach children the "What Should I Wear?" poem at the bottom of the page. Have volunteers match the clothing in the song to the correct picture. (You may wish to add additional verses to include the other clothing from the box.)

6. Then, have children look through the magazines and cut out pictures of clothing. Invite them to glue the pictures to the posters to show the matching weather.

Optional: Invite children to complete the activity master on page 62.

What Should I Wear?

What's the weather like today?
Oh, what should I wear?
If it is sunny and hot,
I'll wear a T-shirt out there!

What's the weather like today?
Oh, what should I wear?
If it is windy and cool,
I'll wear a jacket out there!

What's the weather like today?
Oh, what should I wear?
If it is rainy and warm,
I'll wear a raincoat out there!

What's the weather like today?
Oh, what should I wear?
If it is snowy and cold,
I'll wear mittens out there!

60

Weather Picture Cards

sunny

rainy

windy

snowy

Health, Nutrition, and P.E. PreK–K, SV 141902356X

Name _____ Date _____

What Should I Wear?

1.

2.

3.

4.

 Have children draw lines to match the clothes with the weather.

Unit 1: Health
Health, Nutrition, and P.E. PreK–K, SV 141902356X

Name _____

Date _____

Rosa Stays Well

Rosa knows how to stay well.

1

- - - - - - - - - - - - - Fold - - - - - - - - - - - - -

Activity

What can you do to stay well?
Draw a picture.

Have someone help you write about
the picture.

_____

_____

_____

4

Health, Nutrition, and P.E. PreK–K, SV 141902356X

Rosa brushes her teeth in the morning and before bed. She flosses, too.

Sometimes, Rosa feels stress. She goes for a bike ride to feel better.

2

Rosa tries not to spread germs. She covers her cough.

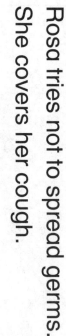

Rosa washes her hands with soap and warm water.

3

Health, Nutrition, and P.E. PreK–K, SV 141902356X

Teacher Resource

Obesity has become a major concern of both children and adults in the United States. The large serving sizes of fast foods combined with a sedentary lifestyle are the prime reasons for increased weight. It is important for children to recognize that they can make choices that will help them live healthy lives. They need to learn the connections between what they eat and the way they look and feel. They need to have the basic information that will help them make good food choices.

The revised food pyramid offers a suggestion for maintaining a healthy lifestyle. Eating the right amount of foods from each group every day provides a balanced diet. Eating too much food from one group or not enough from another can lead to deficiencies or weight problems. Although vitamin supplements can help with these deficiencies, vitamins are best absorbed in the body naturally through the digestion of the foods that contain them.

Nutrition

The body needs to receive certain nutrients in order to grow and to stay healthy. These nutrients are broken down into six types: carbohydrates, proteins, fat, vitamins, minerals, and water.

Carbohydrates are sugars and starches. Sugars, such as fruits and honey, give the body quick energy, while the starches, such as bread, cereal, and rice, give the body stored energy.

Proteins come from foods such as milk, cheese, lean meat, fish, peas, and beans; they help the body to repair itself. Proteins are used by the body to build muscle and bone, and they give the body energy.

Fat is important for energy, too, and it helps to keep the body warm. If the body does not use the fats put into it, it will store the fat. Fats come from foods such as meat, milk, butter, oil, and nuts.

Vitamins are important to the body in many ways. Vitamins help the other nutrients in a person's body work together. Lack of certain vitamins can cause serious illnesses. Vitamin A, for example, which can be obtained from foods such as broccoli, carrots, and liver, helps with eyesight. Vitamin B, from green leafy vegetables, eggs, and milk, helps with growth and energy.

Minerals can be found in foods such as milk, vegetables, seafood, and raisins. They help the body grow. Calcium is a mineral that helps make strong bones, and iron is a mineral needed for healthy red blood.

Water makes up most of the human body and helps to keep the body's temperature regulated. People should drink several glasses of water each day.

The Food Pyramid

A new food pyramid has recently been approved. Since each person is different in terms of age, sex, and exercise levels, the new food pyramid suggests daily dietary needs based on these characteristics. The web site www.mypyramid.gov not only gives serving suggestions and caloric intake, but the site also offers a wealth of information, including a reminder to exercise daily. The five food groups plus oils have changed slightly. Point out that the width of the food group stripes on the pyramid suggests how much food a person should choose from each group. Encourage children to choose more foods from the food groups with the widest stripes.

Grains are made from plants, such as wheat, corn, rice, oats, and barley. Servings of grains are given in ounces.

Vegetables include the plants as well as 100 percent juice. They can be served in any manner, raw or cooked. There are five subgroups: dark green, orange, dry beans and peas, starch, and other vegetables. The serving size for vegetables is given in cups.

Fruits, like vegetables, can be fresh, canned, or 100 percent juice. Eating a wide variety of colorful fruits is highly recommended. Serving sizes are also in cups.

Oils are to be used sparingly. We all need some oil. Oils are found in butter, margarine, nuts, fish, and liquid oils such as corn, soybean, canola, and olive oil. Serving sizes are given in teaspoons.

Milk includes such foods as milk, cheese, yogurt, and ice cream. Skim and low-fat products are recommended to reduce the oil intake. Servings are given in cups.

Meat and Beans include fish, poultry, beef, eggs, nuts, and dried beans, such as navy beans and kidney beans. Serving sizes are given in ounces.

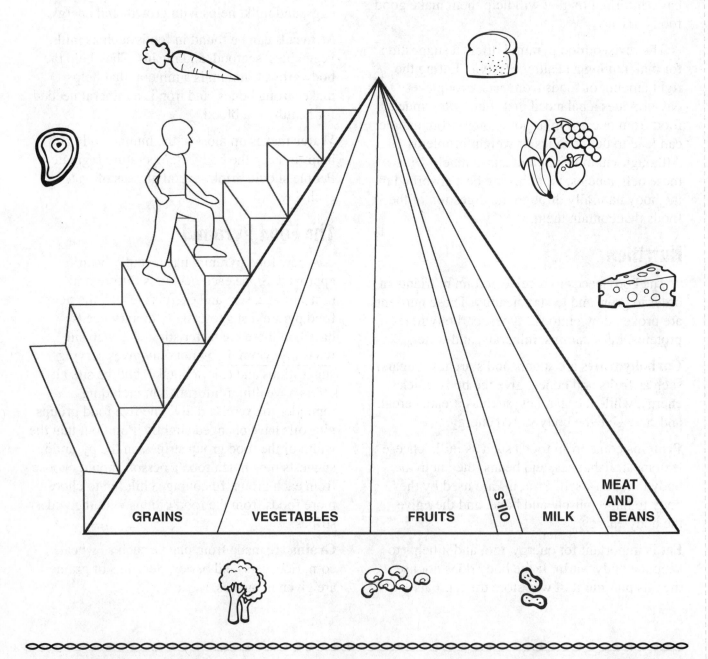

GRAINS   VEGETABLES   FRUITS   OILS   MILK   MEAT AND BEANS

Health, Nutrition, and P.E. PreK–K, SV 141902356X

Nutrition Books

Eat Healthy, Feel Great by M. William Sears (Little, Brown and Company)

Eating the Alphabet: Fruits & Vegetables from A to Z by Lois Ehlert (Harcourt Brace)

Eat Your Vegetables! Drink Your Milk! by Alvin Silverstein (Scholastic)

Good Enough to Eat: A Kid's Guide to Food and Nutrition by Lizzy Rockwell (HarperCollins)

Gregory, The Terrible Eater by Mitchell Sharmat (Scholastic)

Growing Vegetable Soup by Lois Ehlert (Voyager Books)

The Hungry Little Boy by Joan W. Blos (Simon & Schuster Books for Young Readers)

The Little Red Hen by Paul Galdone (Houghton Mifflin Company

Lunch by Denise Fleming (Henry Holt & Company)

Mouse Mess by Linnea Asplind Riley (Scott Foresman)

The Seven Silly Eaters by Mary Ann Hoberman (Browndeer Press)

Stone Soup by Marcia Brown (Simon and Schuster)

Tops and Bottoms by Janet Stevens (Harcourt Children's Books)

The Very Hungry Caterpillar by Eric Carle (Scholastic)

       Health, Nutrition, and P.E. PreK–K, SV 141902356X

Bulletin Board: Keeping Track of Good Food

Materials

food pyramid pattern (page 69)   craft paper   border
engine and train car patterns (page 70)   crayons   scissors
construction paper   tape   stapler

Teacher Directions

1. Prepare a bulletin board with the desired color of craft paper. Add a border and the title "Keeping Track of Good Food."
2. Enlarge and trace the food pyramid on white craft paper. Color and cut out the pyramid.
3. Duplicate an engine and several train cars on different colors of construction paper for each child. You may wish to cut them out for children.
4. Staple the pyramid in the center of the board. Label each section.
5. Staple the completed trains to the board in a pleasing arrangement. Leave room between the trains so that children can add cars. You may wish to accordion pleat the trains as you staple them to allow for more room.

Student Directions

1. Write your name on an engine.
2. Color pictures of the foods you ate last on a train car.
3. Tape the train car to the engine.
4. Get a new car every day. Color the food you eat. Tape the car to your train to keep track of good food.

Health, Nutrition, and P.E. PreK–K, SV 141902356X

Food Pyramid Pattern

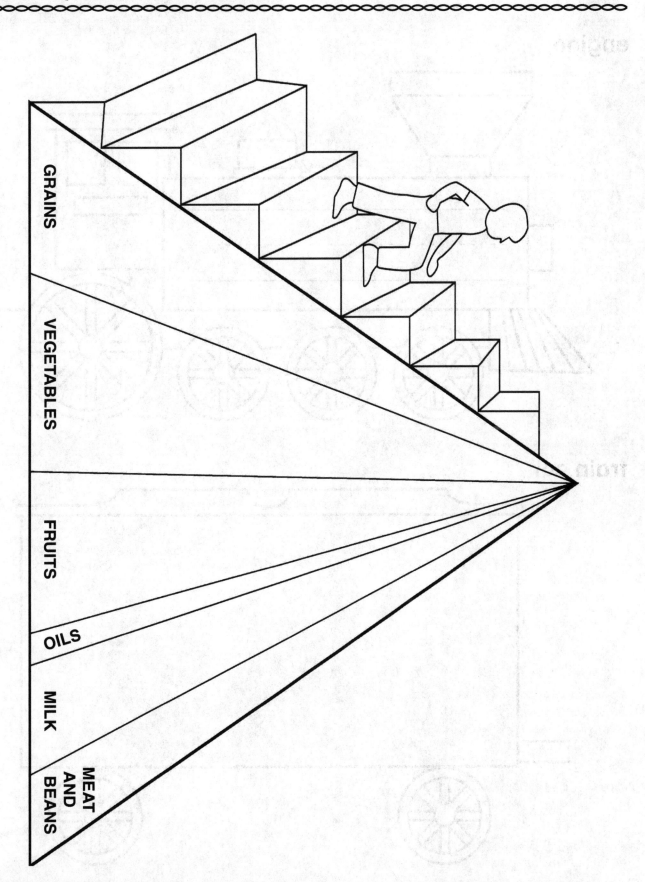

GRAINS

VEGETABLES

FRUITS

OILS

MILK

MEAT AND BEANS

Health, Nutrition, and P.E. PreK–K, SV 141902356X

Engine and Train Car Patterns

engine

train car

Health, Nutrition, and P.E. PreK–K, SV 141902356X

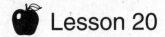 **Lesson 20**

Food and Energy

Standards

- Identifies and practices personal health habits that help individuals stay healthy
- Identifies types of foods that help the body grow

You Need

- battery-operated toy with a battery

Do This

1. Remove the battery from the toy without children seeing. Hide the battery so that it is within easy reach.

2. Display the toy and talk about it.

3. Attempt to turn the toy on. Elicit suggestions from children about why it won't move.

4. Check the battery when it is suggested. Explain that the toy moves because the battery gives it energy.

5. Discuss that food is like a battery for people—it gives them energy to move.

6. Invite children to move with a lot of energy or a little energy at your direction.

7. Discuss activities that take a lot of energy and those that take a small amount of energy. Point out that all activities take energy, but ones that are harder and faster take more energy.

8. Teach children the "Food Gives Me Energy" poem at the bottom of the page.

Optional: Invite children to complete the activity master on page 72.

Food Gives Me Energy

I like to run. I like to play.
Food gives me energy to move this way.
I like to sleep. I like to read.
Food still gives me all the energy I need.
Eating good food is right, I know—
The better I eat, the faster I go!

Name _____ Date _____

A Lot of Energy

🍎 Have children color the pictures of activities that take a lot of energy.

Unit 2: Nutrition
Health, Nutrition, and P.E. PreK–K, SV 141902356X

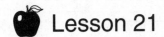 **Lesson 21**

The Food Pyramid

Standards

- Identifies and practices personal health habits that help individuals stay healthy
- Identifies types of foods that help the body grow

You Need

- food pyramid pattern (page 69)
- chart paper
- white construction paper
- scissors
- envelopes
- recycled magazines
- scissors
- tape
- crayons or markers

Do This

1. Enlarge the food pyramid and trace it on chart paper to make a poster. Color and label the sections.

2. Duplicate the food pyramid on white construction paper for pairs of children. Color the pyramids and cut them into sections to make puzzles. Place them in envelopes.

3. Display the food pyramid poster and discuss it with children. Ask questions that help them notice the food groups and the differently sized sections. Explain that the size of the section shows them which foods they should eat more of.

4. Challenge partners to put the food pyramid puzzles together.

5. Teach children the "On the Food Pyramid" song at the bottom of the page. Have children point to the matching section on the puzzle as the food is named. You may wish to add other verses identifying different foods.

6. Next, have children cut out pictures of food from magazines. Have them tape each food in the correct section of the food pyramid poster.

Optional: Invite children to complete the activity master on page 74.

On the Food Pyramid

(Sung to "The Farmer in the Dell")

Bread is a grain.
Bread is a grain.
On the food pyramid,
Bread is a grain.

Other verses:
Peas are a vegetable.
Apples are a fruit.
Butter is an oil.
Cheese is a milk.
Chicken is a meat.

Health, Nutrition, and P.E. PreK–K, SV 141902356X

Name _____ Date _____

The Food Pyramid Match

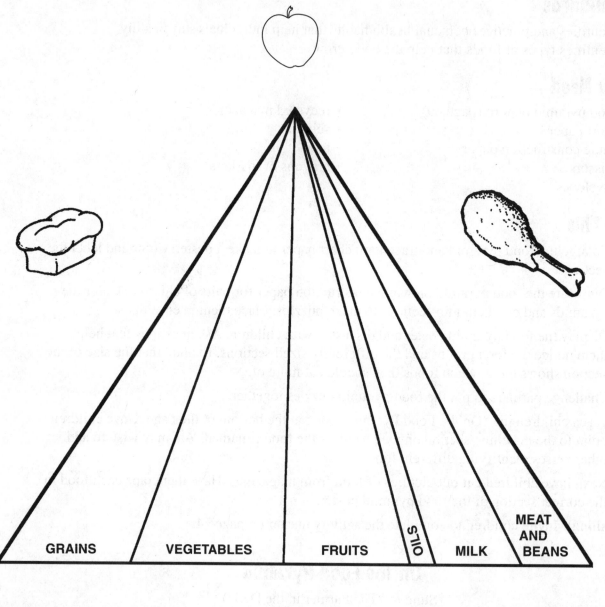

GRAINS   VEGETABLES   FRUITS   OILS   MILK   MEAT AND BEANS

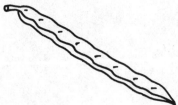

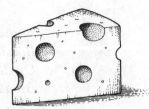

Have children draw a line to match each food to its section of the food pyramid.

Health, Nutrition, and P.E. PreK–K, SV 141902356X

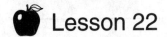 **Lesson 22**

A Healthy Snack

Standards

• Identifies and practices personal health habits that help individuals stay healthy
• Identifies types of foods that help the body grow

You Need

• food pyramid poster (from Lesson 21)
• healthy foods (fruits, vegetables, cereals, cheese, etc.)
• small plates
• forks
• knife

Do This

1. Cut the foods into a variety of shapes, including slices, cubes, and strips. Set them aside on plates.

2. Ask children if they have heard the phrase "You are what you eat." Discuss its meaning.

3. Display the food pyramid poster and discuss healthy food choices and why it is important to eat good food.

4. Teach children the "Hunger Attack" poem at the bottom of the page.

5. Set out the food. Have children identify which food group each belongs to. Then discuss why the foods are healthy choices.

6. Invite children to make a body from the healthy foods they like. For example, a cucumber slice could be a head and carrot strips could be arms.

7. Allow children to eat their snack, reminding them they are what they eat.

Optional: Invite children to complete the activity master on page 76.

Hunger Attack

I like to eat cookies and candy for treats.
But I know that I shouldn't eat too many sweets.
So whenever I get a strong hunger attack,
I reach for a fruit or a vegetable snack!

Name _____ Date _____

Choose Healthy Snacks

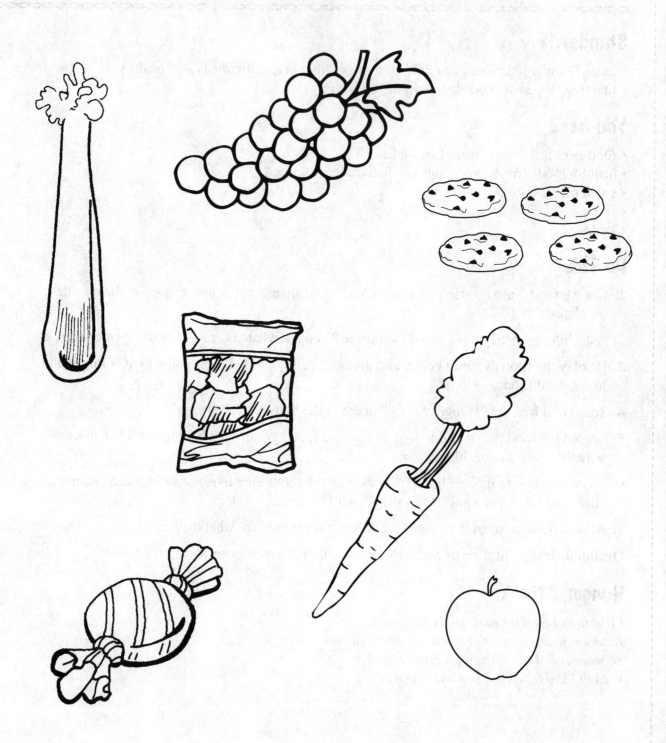

🍎 Have children color the healthy foods they should choose for snacks. Have them cross out less healthy foods.

Unit 2: Nutrition
Health, Nutrition, and P.E. PreK–K, SV 141902356X

Name _____ Date _____

Sandy's Food

Sandy chooses healthy snacks.
She likes fruit.

1

- - - - - - - - - - - - - - Fold - - - - - - - - - - - - - -

Activity

Circle two healthy snacks you like.

Have someone write the names of
your favorite snacks.

_____

_____

_____

4

www.harcourtschoolsupply.com
© Harcourt Achieve Inc. All rights reserved.

77

Unit 2: Nutrition
Health, Nutrition, and P.E. PreK–K, SV 141902356X

Sandy's body needs energy from food.
Her body needs energy at school.

Her body needs energy to play.

2

The Food Pyramid

GRAINS VEGETABLES FRUITS OILS MILK MEAT AND BEANS

The food pyramid helps Sandy choose healthy snacks.

3

Unit 2: Nutrition
Health, Nutrition, and P.E. PreK–K, SV 141902356X

Teacher Resource

Exercising has many healthful benefits. First, muscles grow when they are used. Unexercised muscles contract when they are not used. Muscles that become unaccustomed to exercise can be injured by sudden or strenuous activity. This is why muscles, including the heart, should be exercised regularly and in moderation. Occasional strenuous activity is not advantageous to the muscles and does not give long-term results.

Moreover, exercise also controls weight and increases endurance and strength. Regular exercise can also relax the body, reduce stress, and help people get a good night's sleep. Finally, exercise can reduce the rate of premature mortality from heart disease, hypertension, and colon cancer.

Since schools are often financially restricted, the physical education curriculum is considered less important. The classroom teacher must provide rich and varied experiences for children so they can exercise as well as learn how to establish and maintain a healthy lifestyle. Teachers are responsible for developing a wide variety of activities that promote basic movement skills; games for individuals, partners, and teams; physical fitness; and dance. Teachers also need to ensure that each child achieves his or her optimum mental, emotional, social, and physical development. This is a tall order when the curriculum is already packed with the need to teach core subjects.

The activities and ideas below offer some fun, creative ways to enrich your physical education program, while developing important health goals.

Individual

Letter Jump   Write the alphabet or numbers on index cards and tape them securely to the floor. Call out one locomotive skill (hop, jump, walk, run) and have children find and move to that card. (Children can move in order or to a skill, such as to the card that has the beginning sound or even or odd number pattern.)

Simon Says Body   Make sure children can accurately identify left and right. Then call out left and right body parts that children must touch on themselves. For example, children might touch left elbow to right ankle, or right ear to right foot. Challenge children to be creative in their movements, and remind them they can sit or stand to accomplish the task.

Pattern Moving   Call out actions quickly, such as *Clap your hands* or *Jump on the right foot.* Children complete each movement. Gradually increase the number of instructions that children follow so that they are making four or five movements in a row.

79

The Bouncing Beat   Invite children to choose a ball. Then play different music selections that have a strong beat. Point out the rhythm in each. Challenge children to dribble or drop and catch the ball to the beat. During transition to other music, you may wish to invite children to try different kinds of creative dribbling, such as bounce and spin once, or behind the back.

Pairs or Small Groups

Mirror Me   Have partners face each other. One child is the "image" and the other is the "reflection." The image moves in different ways for the reflection to mirror. Remind children to move slowly to stay in unison.

On a Roll   Cover a box with craft paper and label each side with a body part. Working in small groups sitting in circles, children take turns rolling the box and designating which parts to touch to the floor.

Squirrel Races   Crumple one brown sack for each child. Then spread the sacks on the floor in the middle of the play area. Place a box at each end of the room. Remind children that squirrels often store acorns so they have food during the cold winter months. Then divide the class into two teams and place a team on each side of the play area. Explain that the sacks are acorns, the box is the storage area, and the children will be the squirrels. Tell children they must take turns running to an acorn and picking it up with their chin. Then, they carry the acorn back to the box and drop it in the storage area. No hands are permitted. The first team that has each squirrel successfully retrieve an acorn wins.

Station to Station   Set up a variety of fun activity stations. You might include balls, ropes, hoops, and even tricycles! Then divide the class into groups of four or five. Make one less group than the number of stations. Come up with creative activities children can do while in the stations. Keep the time short so children have to organize and begin the activity quickly.

The Hungry Caterpillar   Gather four of a variety of items, such as small balls, books, or paper clips. Try to get at least eight different items. Spread the items out in a large, cleared area on the floor. Then divide the class into four caterpillar teams. Have them stand in line, one behind the other, and use the left or right hand to hold the shoulder of the person in front. The first person is the "head" of the caterpillar, and the last person is the "tail." Give the tail a plastic grocery sack. On a designated signal, have each caterpillar team move around the floor collecting one of each item in a set amount of time. The head must pick up each item and pass it down the line to the tail. Children cannot disconnect, or all the items

Health, Nutrition, and P.E. PreK–K, SV 141902356X

in the bag must be removed and the team starts again. The first team to gather all the items yells "butterfly."

Hoop Toss   Play this game in a gym or on a field. Designate a row with spots on the floor. Make sure there are at least two hoop diameters between the spots for safety. Give partners a hoop and a ball. One partner stands on the spot and holds the hoop. The other partner stands three feet away and tosses the ball into the hoop. The person with the hoop can position the hoop in any way or move in any direction to catch the ball as long as one foot stays on the spot. After each successful toss, the person with the ball takes one giant step back. The goal is see how far apart partners can move while still successfully tossing the ball into the hoop. Partners switch roles on a miss.

Large Group

Music Statues   Have children dance to music. Encourage them to move to the beat. When the music stops, children freeze in their position. Any child who moves must sit down.

Parachute Number Change   Assign each child a number. Then have all children hold the edges of a parachute at waist level. Call out two or three numbers. Children having those numbers go under the parachute and exchange places.

On the Hot Seat   Have children sit in a circle on the floor or in chairs. One child sits on the "hot seat" in the middle. Call out any characteristic that could relate to children, for example, children who are wearing green, children whose first name begins with *s*, children whose birthdays are in May, etc. If the descriptor applies to the child, he or she gets up and runs to a seat vacated by another child. The person on the hot seat also tries to find another seat. The child left standing is now on the hot seat.

You're a Star Tag   Cut out stars from yellow paper and tape them securely on the floor. Invite several volunteers to be a "star" and stand on a star cutout. Have the remaining children move to one end of the play area. Tell them they are "rockets." Lead stars in a countdown: "3, 2, 1, blastoff!" The rockets move through the stars to the other side of the play area. Stars must keep one foot on the star while trying to tag the rockets. Each tagged rocket "loses power" and stops. They become stars and select a star to stand on. Play continues until all the rockets have been tagged.

Health, Nutrition, and P.E. PreK–K, SV 141902356X

Fitness Books

Babar's Yoga for Elephants by Laurent de Brunhoff (Harry N. Abrams)

Bearobics: A Hip-Hop Counting Book by Victoria Parker and Vic Parker (Viking Books)

Bunnies and Their Sports by Nancy Carlson (Puffin Books)

The Busy Body Book: A Kid's Guide to Fitness by Lizzie Rockwell (Crown Books for Young Readers)

From Head to Toe by Eric Carle (HarperTrophy)

Hamster Camp: How Harry Got Fit by Teresa Bateman (Albert Whitman & Company)

Let's Exercise! by Alice B. McGinty (Franklin Watts)

My Amazing Body: A First Look at Health and Fitness by Pat Thomas (Barron's Educational Series)

The Pooped Troop by Judy Delton (Yearling)

SPORTSercise! by Kim Gosselin (Jayjo Books)

Staying Healthy: Let's Exercise by Alice B. McGinty (PowerKids Press)

Tiffany Dino Works Out by Marjorie Weinman Sharmat (Simon and Schuster Books for Young Readers)

Health, Nutrition, and P.E. PreK–K, SV 141902356X

Bulletin Board: We're Building Our Fitness!

Materials

Builder Bob pattern (page 84)
toolbox pattern (page 85)
tool patterns (pages 84 and 85)

craft paper
construction paper
markers

scissors
stapler

Teacher Directions

1. Prepare a bulletin board with the desired color of craft paper. Trace and cut out the tools to staple to the board for a border. Add the title "We're Building Our Fitness!"
2. Enlarge and trace Builder Bob on white craft paper. Color and cut out the figure. Staple Builder Bob to the center of the board.
3. Duplicate a toolbox and the three tools for each child. Use a variety of construction paper colors. Cut apart and sort the pieces. You may wish to cut the slits in the toolboxes for children.
4. Staple the toolboxes to the board along the sides and bottom.
5. Have children dictate examples of fitness skills and write each skill on a tool. Then, help children add the tools to their toolbox.

Student Directions

1. Get a paper toolbox. Cut it out. Cut a slit.
2. Decorate the toolbox.
3. Write your name.
4. Cut out a tool. Dictate an example of a fitness skill you did. Have someone record the skill on a tool. Put the tool in your toolbox.

Health, Nutrition, and P.E. PreK–K, SV 141902356X

Builder Bob and Hammer Patterns

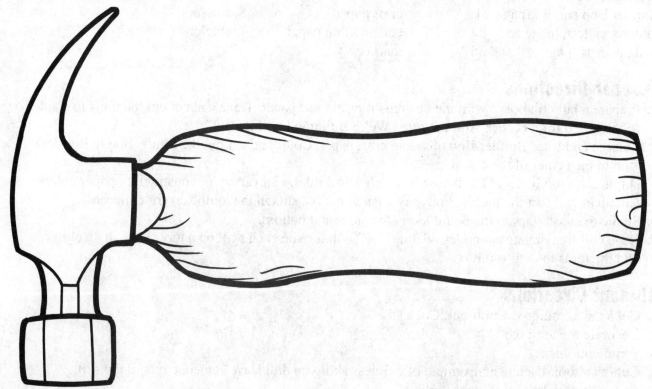

Health, Nutrition, and P.E. PreK–K, SV 141902356X

Toolbox, Screwdriver, and Wrench Patterns

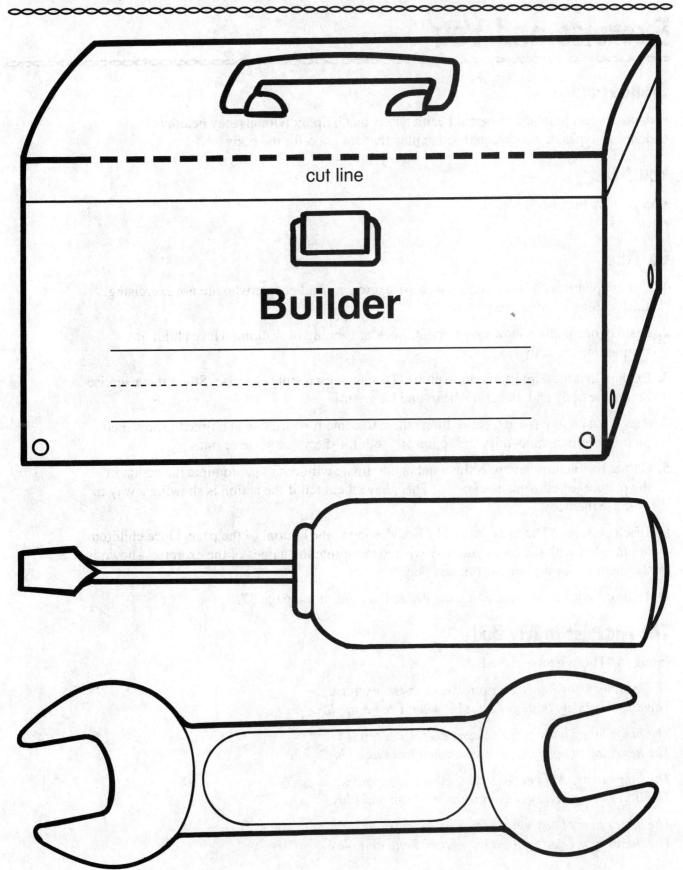

cut line

Builder

Health, Nutrition, and P.E. PreK–K, SV 141902356X

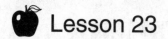 **Lesson 23**

Exercise and You

Standards

• Identifies and practices personal health habits that help individuals stay healthy
• Identifies types of exercise and active play that are good for the body

You Need

• recycled magazines
• scissors

Do This

1. Cut out pictures showing people who are exercising and people who are not exercising. Each child will need one picture.

2. Display one picture showing an action, such as running or walking. Have children pantomime the activity.

3. Explain that the activity shows exercise. Discuss why people exercise. Stress that exercise builds the body and makes the heart and lungs stronger.

4. Pass out a picture to each child. Invite them to come forward one at a time to show their picture. Help them identify the action and tell if it shows exercise or not.

5. Gather the pictures and pass them out again. Invite children to pantomime the action in the picture for classmates to guess. Then, have them tell if the action is showing a way to exercise the body.

6. Teach children "The Muscles in My Body" song at the bottom of the page. Once children are familiar with the song, you may wish to substitute the names of the exercises shown in the pictures for the words "run and play."

Optional: Invite children to complete the activity master on page 87.

The Muscles in My Body

(Sung to "The Wheels on the Bus")

The muscles in my body get exercise, exercise, exercise.
The muscles in my body get exercise when I run and play.

The heart in my body gets exercise, exercise, exercise.
The heart in my body gets exercise when I run and play.

The lungs in my body get exercise, exercise, exercise.
The lungs in my body get exercise when I run and play.

The bones in my body get exercise, exercise, exercise.
The bones in my body get exercise when I run and play.

Who Is Exercising?

🍎 Have children color the pictures that show someone who is exercising.

Health, Nutrition, and P.E. PreK–K, SV 141902356X

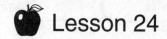 **Lesson 24**

How to Exercise

Standards

• Identifies and practices personal health habits that help individuals stay healthy
• Identifies types of exercise and active play that are good for the body

You Need

• warming up and cooling down picture cards (pages 89 and 90)
• construction paper
• glue

• music player
• slow, relaxing music
• rubber band
• scissors

Do This

1. Enlarge and duplicate the picture cards. Glue them to construction paper. You may wish to laminate them.

2. Play the music and direct children to do one or two of the stretches from the picture cards. Instruct them to hold each for a count of 15.

3. Gather children and explain that they were doing some stretches to warm up the body.

4. Display the rubber band and stretch it several times. Discuss how the muscles are like a rubber band. Explain that stretching the muscles will help keep the body safe when children exercise.

5. Next, show children each picture card and lead them in doing the stretch. Count slowly to 15 to stress the importance of a slow warm-up. Also, explain these rules for proper warm-ups:
   • Never bounce. Stretch gently.
   • Breathe normally to get the air the body needs.
   • Never stretch until it hurts. There should be only a feeling of a slight pull.

NOTE: You may wish to have children exercise at this point.

6. Introduce the phrase *cool down*. Discuss how cooling down is important, too. Invite volunteers to choose a picture card and lead the class in cooling down.

7. Teach children the "This Is the Way We Exercise" song at the bottom of the page.

Optional: Invite children to complete the activity master on page 91.

This Is the Way We Exercise

(Sung to "Here We Go 'Round the Mulberry Bush")

This is the way we warm up, warm up, warm up.
This is the way we warm up before we exercise.

This is the way we work out, work out, work out.
This is the way we work out while we exercise.

This is the way we cool down, cool down, cool down.
This is the way we cool down after we exercise.

Health, Nutrition, and P.E. PreK–K, SV 141902356X

Warming Up and Cooling Down Picture Cards

Shoulder and Chest Stretch

Trunk Stretch

Neck Stretch

Sit and Reach Stretch

Unit 3: P.E.
Health, Nutrition, and P.E. PreK–K, SV 141902356X

Warming Up and Cooling Down Picture Cards

Calf Stretch

Upper Back and
Shoulder Stretch

Thigh Stretch

Calf Stretch

Unit 3: P.E.
Health, Nutrition, and P.E. PreK–K, SV 141902356X

Name _____ Date _____

I Know How to Exercise!

_____
- - - - - - - - -
_____

work out

_____
- - - - - - - - -
_____

warm up

_____
- - - - - - - - -
_____

cool down

🍎 Have children order the steps to show a safe workout.

Unit 3: P.E.
Health, Nutrition, and P.E. PreK–K, SV 141902356X

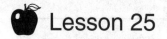 Lesson 25

Safety Equipment

Standards

- Identifies and practices personal health habits that help individuals stay healthy
- Identifies types of exercise and active play that are good for the body
- Identifies the purpose of protective equipment

You Need

- safety equipment (life vest, helmets from different sports, mouth guards, knee and elbow pads, shin guards)

Do This

1. Show children all of the safety equipment. Ask them to guess what the pieces of safety equipment have in common. Guide children to realize the pieces are examples of equipment that keeps people who exercise safe.

2. Have children identify the sport in which each piece of equipment is used.

3. Have volunteers model how to wear the pieces of equipment.

4. Teach children the "Keep Your Body Safe" song at the bottom of the page.

Optional: Invite children to complete the activity master on page 93.

Keep Your Body Safe

(Sung to "The Muffin Man")

Do you keep your body safe, your body safe, your body safe?
Do you keep your body safe when you exercise?

Do you wear an orange life vest, an orange life vest, an orange life vest?
Do you wear an orange life vest when you take a swim?

Other verses:
Do you wear a bike helmet . . . when you ride your bike?
Do you wear two shin guards . . . when you play soccer?
Do you wear elbow pads . . . when you roller-skate?

Name _____ Date _____

Safety First

🍎 Have children color the safety equipment that each child is wearing.

Health, Nutrition, and P.E. PreK–K, SV 141902356X

Name _____

Date _____

Ben Likes to Exercise

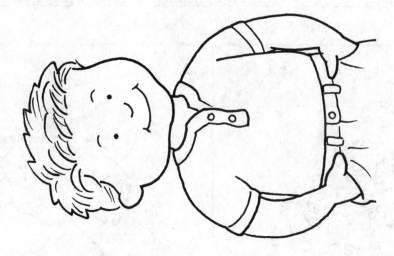

Ben likes to exercise.
He knows what to do.

1

----- Fold -----

Activity

What do you like to do for exercise?
Draw a picture.

Have someone write the name of your exercise.

_____

4

94

Health, Nutrition, and P.E. PreK–K, SV 141902356X

Ben likes to play soccer.
He wears shin guards.
The shin guards keep his body safe.

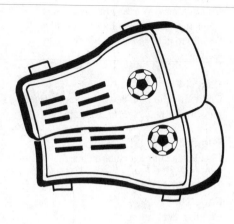

Ben stretches to warm up.

2

Ben plays soccer to work out.

Ben walks to cool down.
Then he stretches again.

3

Unit 3: P.E.
Health, Nutrition, and P.E. PreK–K, SV 141902356X

Answer Key

Page 12
Children may color any of the pictures. Then, they draw a picture of something they do to help change uncomfortable feelings.

Page 14
Children write each body part name. Then, they draw a line to each part on the girl.

Page 16
Check that children color the parts correctly.

Page 20
Children draw a line from:
skull to head.
ribs to chest.
spine to center of body.
foot bones to foot.
arm bones to arm.

Page 22
1. Children color the bike rider who is wearing a helmet.
2. Children color the child who is eating the sandwich.
3. Children color the child who is sleeping.
4. Children color the child who is reading.

Page 28
Answers may vary. Most likely answers are given.
1. Children draw a line to the hand.
2. Children draw a line to the nose.
3. Children draw a line to the ear.
4. Children draw a line to the eye.
5. Children draw a line to the mouth.

Page 30
Children cross out the boy rubbing his eyes, the boy looking at the sun, and the boy using tools without goggles.

Page 32
Answers will vary.

Page 34
1. Children circle the cat.
2. Children circle the rock.
3. Children circle the alligator.
4. Children circle the spoon.

Page 36
Children color the pictures of the doctor and girl, and the girl washing her ear.

Page 38
Answers may vary. Most likely answers are given.
1. salty
2. sweet
3. sour
4. bitter

Page 43
Children write each word. Then, they draw a line to each part of the tooth.

Page 45
Children color the pictures of the girl having her teeth flossed, the girl brushing, and the boy dressed in football clothing.

Page 47
Children color the pictures of the boy putting on sunscreen, the girl washing her hair, and the girl using a nailbrush.

Page 50
Children cross out the pictures of the girl sneezing and the boy coughing without covering their mouth.

Page 53
Answers will vary.

Page 56
Children write their name.

Page 59
Children connect the dots and trace 911.

Page 62
1. Children draw a line to the windy scene.
2. Children draw a line to the rainy scene.
3. Children draw a line to the sunny scene.
4. Children draw a line to the snowy scene.

Page 72
Children color the pictures of the boy riding the bike, the boy running, and the girl jumping rope.

Page 74
Children draw a line from the bread to grains, the bean to vegetables, the apple to fruits, the butter to oils, the cheese to milk, and the chicken to meats and beans.

Page 76
Children color the celery, grapes, carrot, and apple. They cross out the cookies, candy, and chips.

Page 87
Children color the baseball player, swimmer, biker, and soccer player.

Page 91
Children order the pictures 2, 1, 3.

Page 93
1. Children color the life vest.
2. Children color the helmet, knee pads, and elbow pads.
3. Children color the helmet.
4. Children color the shin guards.

Answer Key
Health, Nutrition, and P.E. PreK–K, SV 141902356X